Original title:
Laughs Beneath the Leaves

Copyright © 2025 Creative Arts Management OÜ
All rights reserved.

Author: Julian Prescott
ISBN HARDBACK: 978-1-80567-282-1
ISBN PAPERBACK: 978-1-80567-581-5

Beneath the Boughs of Merriment

Chasing shadows, we run wild,
Laughter spills, a giddy child.
Tickling grass beneath our feet,
Silly sounds, oh what a treat!

Up above, the branches sway,
Whispers of fun come out to play.
With each twist, a giggle grows,
Nature's charm in jest bestows.

Flutters of Fun in the Foliage

Winds that tease and leaves that twirl,
We dance and spin, laugh and whirl.
A crow that caws, a squirrel prance,
Nature's game, the sweetest chance.

Underneath the vibrant shade,
We craft our jokes in laughter made.
Petals drop with shy delight,
A symphony of joy takes flight.

Vibrant Vignettes of Joy under the Trees

In a circle, stories flow,
Whimsical thoughts in ebb and glow.
The breeze plays tricks, says, 'Look and see!'
As we chuckle, so wild, so free.

Sunlight flickers, shadows tease,
Every rustle brings us ease.
With puns that flutter like a bee,
Life is a joke, we laugh with glee.

Outbursts of Delight in the Leafy Dreamland

Acorns drop like silly bombs,
Nature's laughter, oh, what calms!
The giggles bloom like wildflowers,
In this wonder, we spend hours.

Every branch, a tale unfurls,
Jokes exchanged like precious pearls.
In this land where whimsy gleams,
We dance alive, embracing dreams.

Mirage of Mirth Amidst the Maples

In the glade where shadows dance,
Squirrels plot a wild romance.
Acorns drop like laughter's sound,
Giggling echoes all around.

Breezes tickle leafy tips,
Nature joins the playful quips.
Whimsical whispers float and swirl,
As lighthearted pranks unfurl.

Branches sway with jest so bright,
Hosting tales of pure delight.
Dancing leaves in playful pairs,
Grown-ups turned to kids in flares.

Underneath the canopy,
A tapestry of glee we see.
Every twist and turn brings cheer,
A forest filled with love and beer!

Joyfulness in the Arboreal Air

Chirping birds with silly songs,
Flitting by where laughter throngs.
Sunshine filters through the green,
A merrier world than we've seen.

Bouncing bunnies leap with grace,
Each hop brings a smiling face.
Widgets whisper tales absurd,
In forest realms, where joy's not blurred.

Clouds above made of cotton candy,
Swaying branches make it dandy.
Sips of sunshine, tastes of joy,
Nature's thrills are here to enjoy.

With each rustle, secrets spread,
In this playground, we are fed.
Giggles sneak from tree to tree,
The essence of pure jubilee.

Mischief Among the Blossoms

Petals flutter with delight,
Giggly buds in springtime light.
Dandelions play hide and seek,
Jokes shared softly, no need to speak.

Buzzing bees with silly flair,
Middle of mischief, unaware.
Crickets chirping in a band,
Tickling toes on the warm, soft sand.

Underneath the vine and flower,
Cheeky games of giggle power.
Every rustle, every sound,
Blooming laughter flows around.

Chasing shadows, racing sun,
In this realm, we've just begun.
With each chuckle, nature sings,
Silky threads of joy it brings.

Abundant Grins in the Glorious Green

In the emerald depths of cheer,
Nature's gags bring warmth so near.
Tall trees share their tallest jokes,
While giggling roots play with folks.

Fluffy clouds drift in the sky,
Grinning down as they go by.
Whirling leaves on the warm breeze,
Swirling tales that bend the knees.

Gleeful sprouts with outlook bright,
Join together day and night.
Wit and whimsy in the air,
Every breath, a joy to share.

In this forest, smiles unfold,
Stories of laughter gently told.
Amongst the branches, life's a play,
Forever in this merry sway.

Delights of Nature Under the Boughs

Squirrels waltz with acorns in tow,
A dance of footfalls with quite a show.
Birds chirp secrets in giggling tones,
While rabbits giggle on mossy stones.

The sun peeks through with a playful grin,
As shadows chase one another to win.
Crickets play tunes that make you sway,
While butterflies tease in a bright ballet.

Whimsy in the Wilderness Garden

Daisies laugh in their polka-dot dress,
While bees play tag in a busy mess.
The wind tells tales as it rustles the ferns,
With whispers of joy that the heart yearns.

A frog leaps high in a carnival show,
The mushrooms cheer, putting on a glow.
With every step, the world seems to grin,
Nature's antics, let the fun begin!

Playtime in the Leafy Labyrinth

In the thicket where shadows blend,
Foxes play hide and seek 'round the bend.
Each turn reveals a curious sight,
Of giggling critters in the soft twilight.

The trees swirl with laughter, branches entwined,
As whispers of mirth dance in the wind, unconfined.
A patchwork of colors, a joyful display,
Where the echoes of fun never fade away.

Radiant Rejoicing in the Woods

Sunbeams flicker like laughter anew,
As chipmunks scamper with antics in view.
The brook burbles tunes of pure delight,
Reflecting the joy of the warm summer night.

Breezes blow softly, swaying the trees,
Carrying giggles and whispers with ease.
In the heart of the forest, smiles intertwine,
In a jolly mosaic where spirits align.

Mirth Beneath the Arbor

In the shade where giggles dwell,
Squirrels dance like they can tell.
With every rustle, secrets fly,
Leaves whisper laughs as breezes sigh.

Sunbeams tickle the playful breeze,
Flowers nodding to the teasing trees.
Laughter bubbles in sunlit rays,
Nature's jesters hold their sway.

A bumblebee with a wobbly flight,
Buzzing jokes from morning till night.
Under the boughs, silly shadows play,
In this realm of joy, we love to stay.

Smiles Within the Green Embrace

Beneath the canopy so bright,
Crickets chirp with pure delight.
A squirrel chuckles, hops in glee,
Nature's giggles, wild and free.

Blades of grass tickle toes,
While the soft wind gently blows.
A chorus of frogs croak a tune,
Under the watchful afternoon moon.

Butterflies twirl in a dizzy flight,
Flapping wings that shimmer light.
Every moment wraps in cheer,
In this green embrace, we all draw near.

Echoes of Play Among the Branches

Up in the branches, birds convene,
Cracking jokes that spark the scene.
With each flutter, a chuckle shared,
Echoes of mirth, no one prepared.

The playful breeze spins tales of old,
Of hidden treasures and laughs untold.
A fox peeks out, his eyes alight,
Joining the fun, a merry sight.

Underneath the playful sky,
Nature's laughter lifts us high.
In a world where glee is king,
We dance to the songs the wild ones sing.

The Hidden Tickle of Nature

In the grove where shadows bend,
Tiny critters call each friend.
Leaves sway gently, giggles soar,
Nature's warmth, we all adore.

A rabbit hops with crafty cheer,
Chasing laughter, drawing near.
With every twist, a funny glance,
In this world, we twirl and dance.

Whispers float on the balmy air,
As if the trees plot some wild affair.
Nature's tickle, a secret phrase,
In this joyful spot, we love to gaze.

Cheerfulness in the Cradle of Green

In a meadow where giggles fly,
Squirrels dance and butterflies sigh.
Tickled grass beneath big blue skies,
Nature knows where humor lies.

Jokes whispered on the gentle breeze,
Laughter rings through swaying trees.
Listen close, and you'll overhear,
The chuckles carried far and near.

Frolics in the Sunlit Thicket

Tiny feet racing with glee,
Chasing shadows, wild and free.
Beneath the boughs where mischief dwells,
Every rustle of leaves compels.

Frogs wear crowns in the pond's embrace,
While ants march on in a funny race.
Sunbeams sparkle, gleeful and bright,
Nature's joke is pure delight.

Harmony in the Grove of Laughter

Whispers of joy in rustling leaves,
The breeze carrying playful thieves.
Branches sway with cheerful tunes,
Tickling chins beneath the moons.

Mice in hats tiptoe around,
Surprises waiting to be found.
Giggling shadows on the ground,
In this grove, bliss knows no bounds.

Merriment in the Leafy Sanctuary

In shadows deep, where stories sprout,
A dance of wonder, endless route.
Joyful echoes weave through the scene,
Wonders waiting, quaint and keen.

Crickets sing their nighttime song,
A gathering where all belong.
With every rustle, worlds collide,
In a refuge where laughter resides.

Sunlight and Smiles in the Arbor

In the shade where shadows play,
Squirrels dance in bright array.
A robin sings a silly song,
While the breeze joins in along.

Laughter echoes, branches sway,
As sunlight giggles through the day.
A butterfly spins in delight,
Tickling flowers, oh what a sight!

Beneath the boughs, friends gather near,
Telling tales, sharing cheer.
A ant in a suit, oh so proud,
Makes the children laugh out loud!

In every rustle and every croak,
The trees themselves seem to joke.
Nature's party, oh what a tease,
Joyful moments drift on the breeze.

Frolics in the Forest's Embrace

A fox with a hat on its head,
Scurries fast, magic instead.
With twinkling eyes and nimble paws,
It winks at the deer, just because!

Underneath the leafy dome,
Creatures gather, far from home.
A bear in boots, it trips and rolls,
Filling the air with howling yowls!

The mushrooms laugh with spotted caps,
As giggles bounce in gentle laps.
A frog in a tie plays jump rope,
Casting shadows, giving hope.

Laughter springs from every tree,
The forest sings in harmony.
A parade of whimsy, all in glee,
Nature's jesters, wild and free.

Humorous Tales of Trellis and Tree

In the garden where laughter grows,
A snail in shades takes it slow.
A cunning raccoon, with a quirky grin,
Digs for treasures that lie within.

Vines whisper secrets, soft and low,
As daisies chuckle, row by row.
A hedgehog trips, then laughs at its fate,
Rolling round as if on a plate!

The sunflowers sway, tall and bright,
While a caterpillar dances in flight.
Together they share stories and jokes,
Enticing joy from all the folks.

With a twirl and a spin, the flowers cheer,
As petals flutter, drawing near.
In this patch of green, so full of fun,
Nature's humor can't be outdone!

Cheerful Harmonies of Flora and Fauna

In the meadow where colors blend,
A hare hops in with joy to send.
Bumblebees buzz a merry tune,
As daisies dance beneath the moon.

The tree trunks chuckle, deep and wise,
Watching antics beneath the skies.
A parrot squawks, "You look like me!"
While frogs compete in a croaking spree.

Each leaf shivers with laughter's grace,
As chipmunks race, a wild chase.
A whimsical drama unfolds and plays,
In nature's theater, a joyful craze.

Together in harmony, bright and warm,
Flora and fauna, a magical charm.
In this world where fun will stay,
Every heartbeat echoes, "Let's play!"

Whimsy from the Woodland Whispers

In a grove where squirrels vie,
A rabbit hops with a winked eye.
Dance and prance, oh what a jest,
Nature's stage is truly best.

The chipmunk giggles, tells a tale,
Of lost acorns doomed to fail.
The branches sway with soft delight,
As shadows play in dappled light.

Frogs croak puns near the stream,
While dragonflies dart and gleam.
A deer trips on roots, oh dear!
But laughter fills the woodland sphere.

Mushrooms chuckle, sprouting wide,
In this playground, none can hide.
Every moment brings a joke,
In this forest, smiles provoke.

Jests among the Twisting Vines

Vines entwined in playful loops,
With tiny critters forming troops.
A chubby mouse slips on a leaf,
Bringing forth the best of brief.

A parrot squawks a silly rhyme,
As butterflies dance, keeping time.
They frolic in the sunny rays,
Sharing joy in merry ways.

A turtle humorously strolls,
Through flower beds, it gently trolls.
Each step a little comedic thrill,
Nature's humor, a perfect spill.

Among the vines, the laughter swells,
With chirps and giggles, all is well.
Here, the whispers never pause,
Life's a jest dressed as applause.

Giggles Rocking in the Breeze

The breezes carry giggles bright,
Through leaves that shimmer in the light.
Each blade dances as if to tease,
Whispers play on all the trees.

Beneath the branches, shadows gleam,
A playful crow joins in the theme.
It caws a joke, then takes to flight,
Chasing whispers, oh what a sight!

A laughing fox peers from behind,
With mischief dancing in its mind.
It trips on roots, then gives a wink,
In this realm, we never think.

Sunbeams splash with vibrant hues,
While nature laughs, we share the news.
In every rustle, in every sway,
The world's a stage where we can play.

Enchantment Among the Leafy Boughs

In leafy crowns, the magic spins,
While hidden critters hide their grins.
A rabbit serves a playful jest,
Skipping 'round in joyous quest.

The woodpecker knocks, a funny beat,
While daisies sway beneath our feet.
A raccoon peeks with playful eyes,
As sunlight dances, laughter flies.

Bats above do graceful twirls,
While squirrels share their acorn pearls.
Under boughs where spirits dance,
Every glance is a merry chance.

With stolen moments, hearts take flight,
The woodland hums with pure delight.
Here, in whispers, joy is found,
In every leaf, love's laughter's loud.

Giggles Among the Garden's Glisten

In the garden where daisies sway,
Little critters come out to play.
A squirrel wearing socks with flair,
Steals the scene with a silly stare.

Bumblebees buzzing their little tune,
Tickle the flowers in bright afternoon.
A frog with a hat sings loudly near,
While the daisies dance, bringing cheer.

Chasing shadows, the children squeal,
Dancing lightly with zest and zeal.
In this haven where happiness thrives,
Joyful whispers stir up our lives.

A butterfly takes a comedic flight,
Mocking the clouds with pure delight.
In laughter's embrace, we find our place,
As giggles bloom in the sunlit space.

A Serenade of Smiles and Sunbeams

Sunshine drips like golden honey,
Tickling noses, oh so funny.
The grass grows tall, a jolly sight,
Inviting frolic from morning to night.

A jester robin hops on one leg,
Dancing on branches, a lively peg.
Nearby, a tortoise wearing shades,
Mimics cool cats in leafy glades.

Ticklish vines curl around the fence,
Making nature's laughs feel immense.
With each breeze, a playful tease,
As the petals flutter with such ease.

Butterflies laugh with a fluttered cheer,
Whispering secrets for all to hear.
In this moment, mirth takes the lead,
As smiles and sunbeams plant joyous seeds.

Heartfelt Joys Whistling through Willows

Amidst the willows, laughter springs,
Where chattering birds give joyfully sings.
A hedgehog prances in silly shoes,
Dodging winks from the playful muse.

Whistles of winds weave through the trees,
Tickling the hearts with whimsical ease.
The daisies are giggling in soft delight,
While mischievous shadows come out at night.

A family of ducks in a waddling line,
With antics that simply look divine.
In muddy puddles, a splash brings glee,
As laughter bubbles like petals on spree.

Every moment, a spark to ignite,
As joy dances free in the warm twilight.
With every tune that the willows hum,
Life sings of brilliance, oh, what fun!

Mischievous Murmurs in the Mulberry

Under the mulberry, tales unfold,
With whispers of antics both shy and bold.
A raccoon wearing a jester's hat,
Plays peekaboo, imagine that!

Among the branches, giggles rise,
Leaves seem to chuckle, nature's surprise.
A kitten tries to catch a breeze,
Tumbling down in a flurry with ease.

The shadows dance in a playful tune,
While the flowers sway beneath the moon.
Every rustle brings laughter near,
As the night wraps us warm in cheer.

With mischief alight, sparkles in sight,
In this secret garden, hearts take flight.
A chorus of chuckles in the free air,
Murmuring joy, laughter to share.

Joyous Revelry Under the Branches

Beneath the boughs, life dances bright,
The breeze whispers jokes, what a delight.
Squirrels in jest, they scamper and play,
Each twist and turn, in a merry ballet.

Sunbeams flicker, laughter in the air,
Birds chirp songs of fun, without a care.
In this vibrant realm, let your heart soar,
With giggles and grins, who could ask for more?

The rustling leaves share secrets untold,
Of playful pranks, a sight to behold.
Laughter echoes, a sweet serenade,
In this lively grove, all worries will fade.

Gather your friends beneath the green dome,
In this cozy nook, find your true home.
With every chuckle, a bond so divine,
In joyous revelry, may our spirits entwine.

Snickers from the Ancient Oak

In the shade of the oak, stories collide,
Each branch a witness, a giggle to hide.
The squirrels conspire, with mischief in eyes,
As shadows dance lightly, a trick in disguise.

Acorns drop softly, like a thud of a joke,
While whispers of wind, tease the old oak.
A chipmunk's grin, with a dash of glee,
Invites all to join in the jubilee.

With roots intertwined, they spread joy around,
In this whimsical place, laughter resound.
Their chatter a symphony of playful delight,
Beneath the vast branches, all shines so bright.

Echoing chuckles, through each mighty limb,
Every heart gathered, on whimsy does brim.
In nature's embrace, let silly times flow,
By the ancient oak, where snickers bestow.

A Symphony of Smiles in the Forest Hall

In the forest hall, where the wild things roam,
There's a symphony of smiles, calling all home.
The ferns sway gently, to a rhythm so sweet,
Each creature joining in, a dance on their feet.

Bubbles of laughter rise up from the stream,
Where the frogs croak sonnets, like a playful dream.
Mice play tag, racing through the tall grass,
In this joyful theater, worries don't last.

The sunlight beams through, a glimmering show,
Mirth dances lightly, wherever you go.
Owls wink knowingly, from their lofty perch,
With each little chuckle, hearts start to lurch.

Gather round, friends, let the fun be your guide,
In this vibrant space, let joy be your tide.
A symphony of happiness calls from the glen,
Join in the laughter, come back once again.

Mirth Among the Meadowflowers

Where the meadow blooms in colors so bright,
Mirth twirls and twinkles, pure delight.
Butterflies flutter, sipping sweet cheer,
While daisies whisper jokes for all to hear.

Bumblebees buzz in a hap-happy tune,
Tickling the petals beneath the warm noon.
Each flower's expression, a smile to bestow,
In the vibrant light, let the joy overflow.

The path is a canvas, painted with glee,
As critters cavort in a whimsical spree.
Laughter intertwined with the buzzing of bees,
In this garden of giggles, life's simple and free.

So come take a stroll, let your worries unfurl,
Among the meadowflowers, watch fun swirl.
With every bright bloom, and each chuckling breeze,
Find mirth in the moment, let laughter appease.

Lively Laughter Laced in the Leaves

In a realm where shadows play,
The squirrels dance and prance all day,
With acorns flying left and right,
Their antics bring pure delight.

Beneath the boughs, a giggle grows,
The breeze whispers secrets, who knows?
A ticklish tickle from the trees,
Makes everyone laugh, oh with ease!

Frogs leap around in funny hats,
While chatting birds share their spats,
The rustling grass joins in the cheer,
Creating a symphony so clear.

Nature's jesters, wild and free,
Sprinkle joy like confetti, you'll see,
As the sun lights up every face,
In this enchanted, happy place.

Entertaining Echoes Down by the Evergreens

The pines hum tunes of pure delight,
Echoes bouncing, oh what a sight,
The rabbits chuckle as they hop,
Just trying not to make a plop.

Beneath the lush, green canopy,
A tale unfolds quite magically,
Feathered friends in playful flight,
Bring smiles and sparkles, heartily bright.

Crickets chirp their catchy song,
While wandering deer join right along,
Each creature adds their silly flair,
Creating laughter everywhere.

With every rustle, joy does spread,
Nature's stage where fun is fed,
So gather 'round, both young and old,
These moments, truly worth their gold.

Secrets of Sunshine among the Sapphire Sycamores

Under sapphire-studded skies,
Playful secrets in disguise,
The sunbeams chase the shadows away,
As giggles start to win the day.

A crafty fox with a twinkling eye,
Winks at the clouds drifting by,
While chipmunks plan their cheeky games,
Unleashing laughter without names.

The rustling leaves play tag with the breeze,
Tickling every bark and tree with ease,
Nature's humor, bold and bright,
Spreading joy each morning light.

Come one, come all, to the merry scene,
Where all is silly, and nothing's mean,
In this haven of unfiltered cheer,
The magic of fun draws us near.

Frolicsome Spirits in the Fragrant Forest

In fragrant woods where spirits dance,
Harmony blooms with every chance,
The air is filled with joyous shouts,
Echoing the thrill of playful bouts.

Toadstools host a jolly feast,
Where every critter is a guest, at least,
With laughter rising like sweet perfume,
Every corner filled with good-vibe bloom.

The swirling leaves join in the fun,
Casting shadows beneath the sun,
As fireflies twinkle in the air,
Embracing lightness everywhere.

So skip along this cheerful route,
With every flutter, laugh, and shout,
For in this forest, bright and grand,
Joy dances wild, hand in hand.

Jests in the Garden Sanctuary

In the garden where shadows play,
A squirrel juggles nuts all day.
The flowers giggle, petals sway,
As bees buzz dances, come what may.

A rabbit tells a silly joke,
The turtle laughs, nearly broke.
The sun winks down, a friendly poke,
While butterflies sip tea and croak.

Crickets chirp their quirky tune,
As frogs wear hats, they'll be a boon.
With each bright note, the flowers prune,
All creatures bask beneath the moon.

So join the fun, don't shy away,
In a silly world, come frolic and play.
For every turn, there's just delay,
In garden joys, we'll laugh today.

Sprightly Sounds of the Sylvan

In the woods where sunlight beams,
A fox jests in wild, wavy dreams.
The owls chuckle, or so it seems,
While mushrooms hum in goofy themes.

The trees, they gossip, branches sway,
As chipmunks dance in bold ballet.
With every rustle, games at play,
A froggy chorus leads the way.

Squirrels wear capes in playful flight,
And shadows play tricks in the night.
A whispered joke ignites delight,
In this realm, life feels just right.

So roam the paths both wide and narrow,
Catch a giggle—a jolly sparrow.
In this land of whimsical airrow,
Embrace the joy, let laughter harrow.

Glee in the Grove of Laughter

In the grove, where giggles bloom,
A hedgehog crafts a funny room.
With acorns stacked in playful gloom,
The sun beams bright, casting off doom.

A dance-off found within the trees,
As rustling leaves nod with the breeze.
Each critter shows some funky freeze,
Drawing laughter with such ease.

A bird finds joy in funny songs,
As fireflies join, all night long.
The breeze hums soft, where all belongs,
In a magical place, we feel strong.

So come and take a merry seat,
In nature's laughter, life feels sweet.
A jolly vibe in rhythmic beat,
Join in the cheer, let joy repeat.

Tickle of the Wind through Twigs

Beneath the boughs, the whispers sing,
The wind tells tales of spirited spring.
A playful breeze makes branches swing,
   As critters laugh at everything.

A deer, wearing shades, struts with zest,
   Among the leaves, it's simply best.
With each soft rustle, they jest and jest,
In the heart of green, they find their rest.

The rabbits hop with silly flair,
While ants compete, they cannot spare.
   With nature's humor filling air,
Each twist and turn delights with care.

So wander through this cheerful land,
   Where every leaf has fun so grand.
   In the tickle of the wind, we stand,
Embracing joy, both soft and planned.

Giggling through the Greenery

In the shade, where shadows play,
Squirrels dance in a comical way.
Leaves rustle with giggles and cheer,
Nature's humor is always near.

A butterfly lands with a fluttery grace,
Tickles a snail, what a silly race!
They wiggle and wobble, a sight to behold,
In this merry realm, stories unfold.

A rabbit hops with a wink and a nod,
While the old oak tree stands, a wise, happy god.
The wind shares secrets, whispers so light,
In a world full of chuckles, everything's bright.

Echoes of Merriment Among the Foliage

Dancing shadows beneath the sun,
Whispers of joy have just begun.
A fox in a hat, what a curious sight,
Capering around with joy and delight.

Frogs croak jokes from their lily pads,
Laughter erupts, no room for sad.
A tumble of leaves swirls in the air,
Tickling fawns with nibbles to share.

The trees are alive with chuckles and fun,
As critters gather, their antics begun.
Echoes of laughter ring clear and loud,
In this whimsical world, we're all quite proud.

Chuckles in the Woodland Breeze

A jester's hat on a raccoon's head,
He juggles acorns, so silly, so fed.
Laughter floats on the soft, warm air,
As chipmunks giggle without a care.

The brook gurgles a playful tune,
While cheeky birds serenade the moon.
Breezes tickle the branches high,
As all join in on the joyful sigh.

Tiptoeing deer wear masks made of vines,
Join in the fun as nature intertwines.
With every rustle and every croon,
The forest giggles, morning to moon.

Mirth Under the Verdant Veil

Beneath the green, the mischief brews,
With playful shadows and nature's news.
A hedgehog chuckles, prancing about,
While a wise old owl checks it out.

A worm quakes, tickled by a ray,
As it wriggles on its carefree way.
Frolicking fawns leap in delight,
Turning the woods into sheer delight.

Flowers giggle, petals in sway,
As breezes dance and warmly play.
In every leaf, in every sigh,
Laughter thrives beneath the sky.

Lively Frolics in Nature's Nook

In the grove where giggles play,
Squirrels dance the day away.
Chasing shadows, they collide,
Under twigs, they often hide.

Birds with hats on upside down,
Chirp a tune that draws a crowd.
With each leap, a joyful cheer,
Nature's playground, loud and clear.

Bouncing leaves like soft balloons,
Tickled by the sunlit tunes.
Nature's winks and playful glee,
Life is full of jubilee!

In this nook, the world does grin,
Every heart can join the spin.
Lively frolics, pure delight,
In the arms of day and night.

Bubbly Reflections in the Leafy Glens

In the glens, where whispers cheer,
Mirror ponds make mischief near.
Fish that splash and frogs that leap,
With a giggle, secrets keep.

The sun peeks through the leafy maze,
Painting shadows that dance and graze.
Butterflies flit, all aglow,
In this bubbly, lively show.

Ducks with boots and playful styles,
Swim and twirl for joy and smiles.
Every ripple tells a tale,
In the breezes, laughs prevail.

Here in glens, the fun won't cease,
Nature's laughter brings us peace.
Bubbly bliss, we'd never trade,
In this magic, joys cascade.

Ticklish Breezes at the Tree's Heart

Winds that swirl around the trunks,
Wiggle leaves and tease the flunks.
In the branches, whispers sway,
Ticklish breezes come to play.

Rabbits hop with bouncy grace,
Chasing tickles, quick to race.
Breezes giggle as they dash,
Through the thickets, wild and brash.

Branches sway with hearty laughs,
While squirrels draft their cheeky graphs.
Velvet moss invites a sit,
Spinning tales while shadows flit.

At the heart where fun resides,
Nature's joy forever guides.
Ticklish breezes, laugh and glide,
In this haven, we abide.

Serene Snickers in the Sunny Glade

In the sunny glade, we find,
Snickers shared, and joy entwined.
Buttercups and daisies peek,
As if they yearn to play and speak.

Lizards lounging on warm stones,
With their grins and silly tones.
Every rustle, every whim,
Nature's laughter on a whim.

Clouds above look down and smile,
Whispering secrets all the while.
Swishing grasses play along,
In this glade, we all belong.

Serenity with giggles mixed,
A sunny spot where hearts are fixed.
Together in this joyful place,
Nature's snickers, sweet embrace.

Whispers of Joy Amongst the Foliage

In the trees, where shadows play,
Squirrels dance without a care.
With acorns tossed, they shout hooray,
As birds around them chirp and share.

Rustling leaves, a secret tune,
The chubby toad croaks with delight.
Sunbeams filter, a golden boon,
Creating smiles from morning light.

A fox tiptoes, trying to hide,
But trips on roots and starts to spin.
The laughter echoes far and wide,
In this forest, no room for sin.

So come and join the merry crew,
In the magic where joy runs free.
With every rustle, laughter's cue,
Nature's humor, a sight to see.

Giggles Under the Canopy

The breeze tickles the branches high,
While shadows twist and swirl below.
The playful winds, they tease and pry,
As leaves join in the jocund show.

A bunny hops with surprising grace,
Then stumbles, sending petals flying.
With fluffy tail, it picks up pace,
While bugs around it join in trying.

Bright colors flash among the green,
While flowers nod with giggling glee.
The smallest critters weaves the scene,
Creating fun for all to see.

The sun dips low, the day near done,
Yet joyous chuckles still remain.
In the heart of nature's fun,
The laughter dances in the rain.

Serenades in the Shady Grove

In dappled light, the voices bend,
Whispers carried in the shade.
A mouse with cheese, ready to send,
A tune that makes the sun cascade.

A party's brewing, can't you tell?
With twigs that tap like tiny drums.
The creatures gather, quite the swell,
As laughter bubbles, then it hums.

A raccoon jests with playful flair,
Attempts to juggle pinecones round.
Each slip and drop sends up the air,
With snickers shining, joy unbound.

Beneath the boughs, the spirits thrive,
As mirthful echoes fill the air.
In the grove, they come alive,
With every chuckle, all laid bare.

Chortles on the Forest Floor

Underfoot, the mushrooms wiggled,
As tiny feet made merry sighs.
A ladybug, she danced and giggled,
While butterflies spun in the skies.

A raccoon rolled in leafy heaps,
While busy ants took to their task.
With every trip, the forest leaps,
A lively crew, no need to ask.

Crickets chirp a playful tune,
Echoing through the fragrant air.
The fox gives chase, but not too soon,
For finding friends is what they share.

So gather 'round this lively floor,
Where joy is found in every sound.
In nature's midst, forevermore,
Chortles rise, as laughter's found.

Lightness in the Heart of the Woods

The squirrels debate who can leap the best,
While chipmunks giggle at their tiny jest.
Amongst the trees, a parade unfolds,
As patches of sunlight tease, bright and bold.

A raccoon jogs in mismatched shoes,
Scaring poor rabbits, who can't help but snooze.
Their dreams, a circus of acrobatic treats,
In the heart of the woods, such whimsical feats.

The brook, it gurgles with a chuckling sound,
While the old owl hoots, wisdom unbound.
With every rustle, the forest reveals,
A realm where joy and laughter conceal.

Beneath the canopies, mirth goes on,
As nature and creatures share a sweet song.
Where every twig snaps, a giggle is found,
In a lighthearted realm, spun round and round.

Cheer in the Heart of the Hollow

Down in the nook where the shadows play,
A hedgehog winks, oh, what a ballet!
With wobbly spins and clumsy prance,
Distracting the thistle with a silly dance.

The toads on the log croak a jolly tune,
While fireflies boogie under the moon.
A cloud of giggles floats softly around,
As all the sweet creatures gather 'round.

An old fox tells tales of a chicken chase,
With exaggerated leaps, and a fluffed-up face.
They crowd 'round as he gestures and sings,
The cheer of the hollow, where happiness springs.

When a breeze whispers secrets of joy from afar,
The laughter ignites like a dancing star.
In the heart of the hollow, just take a look,
Life is a page from a comical book.

Whispers of Joy in the Canopy

Up in the branches, a gathering's set,
With chattering birds, a laughter duet.
A parrot mimics with a cheeky grin,
As everyone joins in the jubilant din.

The monkeys swing low, with a playful shout,
Turning the dull into something about.
With belly flops from a high swinging vine,
They tumble and tumble, it's laughter divine!

Beneath the bright leaves, secrets unfold,
A family of shadows, their stories retold.
With giggles and whispers, camaraderie flows,
In sweet little pockets, where friendship grows.

Each rustle and chirp echoes happiness true,
As sunlight splashes in whimsical hues.
The canopy dances, light-footed and free,
Creating a tapestry of sheer jubilee.

Secrets Shared in Sunlit Shadows

In the dappling light, where the soft breezes tease,
The garden becomes a stage for the bees.
They buzz with humor, a jolly parade,
While daisies and dandelions wink in the shade.

A snail on a leaf, with a crown made of dew,
Tells tales of adventure, as snails often do.
With floppy defenses and a heart made of cheer,
He shares with his buddies, drawing them near.

The sunbeams cascade in a playful ballet,
Where shadows grow long, in the evening's bouquet.
A meeting of creatures both big and small,
Sharing their secrets beneath the sun's call.

As fireflies twinkle in the twilight's embrace,
The chorus of chuckles swells into space.
In every shadow, a story to weave,
In a realm of delight, where we all can believe.

Dancing Leaves and Delighted Souls

In the gentle breeze, they swirl and play,
Whispering secrets they won't betray.
A happy jig, with twirls and spins,
Nature's laughter, where joy begins.

Squirrel in the branches, with acorn snack,
Cracks a joke, and the world looks back.
The sunlight giggles upon the ground,
While shadows join in, swaying around.

Breezes tickle the vibrant stems,
Jokes shared softly, among the gems.
A wiggly worm in a leafy hat,
Is there a punchline? Well, imagine that!

Oh, the rustling shapes that dance in rhyme,
Every step a chuckle, counted in time.
The forest holds secrets, oh what a tease,
Where a smile grows big, amongst the trees.

A Tapestry of Smiles Amidst the Shrubbery

Amidst the bushes where giggles bloom,
Silly shadows play and thrum.
Each leaf a canvas, bright and bold,
Tales of mirth waiting to be told.

The foxes chuckle, tails in the air,
As they weave through brush without a care.
A raccoon stumbles, gives a surprising shout,
Only to find there's no one about.

Sun-drenched petals burst into glee,
Tickling the toes of a nearby bee.
A playful breeze nudges the flowers' quips,
As laughter dances on fluttering hips.

In every corner, a bright-eyed grin,
Nature rejoices, let the fun begin!
As smiles stitch up a canvas of cheer,
We gather together, year after year.

Hidden Humor in the Arboreal Wisdom

From high up branches, oh, what a sight,
Woodpeckers knock with delight,
Pinecones tumble and roll down fast,
Cracking jokes that forever last.

Swaying together in sun and shade,
Secrets amusedly played and displayed.
A wise old owl with a comedic flair,
Shares tales of mischief with a knowing air.

A chipmunk fumbles, his stash all around,
What a disaster, yet joy knows no bound.
With every rustle, a punchline is found,
In wisdom of trees, laughter resounds.

So listen closely, when nature confides,
There's humor abound where the foliage hides.
In the rustling leaves and the bark's gentle creak,
Echoes of laughter, soft, yet unique.

Cheery Chats in Charmed Grove

In a grove where giggles grow like ferns,
Curious critters take playful turns.
A chatty chipmunk spins tales with flair,
While friendly shadows breathe in the air.

A wise old tree, with a smile so wide,
Echoes the laughter that cannot hide.
Under its branches, a gathering blooms,
Of friends sharing whims amidst nature's tunes.

Grassy patches where daisies peek,
Tickle the toes and make 'em squeak.
A dance of the daisies, a jolly parade,
Where cheer finds a home, nature's serenade.

Through the branches, merriment flows,
Frolicking critters, in their costume shows.
In this enchanted and jovial spree,
We find the joy where we too can be free.

Ticklish Tunes of the Trees

In the shade where shadows play,
The breezes dance, sway and sway.
Squirrels chatter, acorns drop,
Nature's giggles never stop.

Branches jiggle, they can't be still,
Trees around hum with a thrill.
A gust of wind, a creaky sound,
In this joy, we all are bound.

Burbling brooks sing silly songs,
With every ripple, righting wrongs.
Beneath the sky, laughter soars,
In this harmony, our hearts explore.

Tickles found in rustling greens,
Amid the twirls and playful scenes.
Each leaf a note, a vibrant hue,
In nature's band, we join the cue.

Cheerful Rhapsody in the Leafy Domain

In the leafy realm, where giggles rise,
The sun peeks through, a playful disguise.
Frolicking critters join the spree,
In this orchestra, wild and free.

The bushes dance with lively flair,
While dandelions float in the air.
Whispers spread from tree to tree,
Joyful echoes call out, come see!

Beneath the branches, secrets shared,
Every corner, the laughter's bared.
Nature's charm, a lively tune,
In this magic, all feel immune.

Chirping birds, with wings so bright,
Composing melodies of pure delight.
In the leafy domain, we find our muse,
With every chuckle, the world we choose.

Blithe Whispers in the Green Realm

In the green realm, whispers sweet,
Where jocular breezes and laughter meet.
Frogs croak puns by the pond's edge,
The dance of life, a joyful pledge.

Mirthful blooms in colors bold,
Painted stories waiting to be told.
Each rustling leaf a hearty laugh,
A tapestry woven, nature's craft.

In the thicket, the rabbits prance,
With tiny steps, they twist and dance.
The rhythm of nature, fun to hear,
Echoing joy, it's crystal clear.

As shadows play in the golden light,
The world becomes a pure delight.
In these whispers of the wood,
We find the humor, all is good.

Eclectic Elation in the Evergreen

In the evergreen, where spirits soar,
The stories spun, forever more.
Pinecones tumble, laughter spreads,
In secret nooks, where joy treads.

Branching out with quirky tales,
Life unfolds in vibrant trails.
Chirpy insects buzz around,
Playful antics can be found.

A squirrel's leap, a frog's big splash,
Nature's comedy forms a mash.
Through twinkling stars and rustling leaves,
Elation brews in all it weaves.

Moonlight giggles in evening's glow,
Whispers of secrets we all know.
In this haven, spirits blend,
With every chuckle, a cherished friend.

Sunlight's Grin Through the Verdant Veil

Golden rays peek through the trees,
Whispers of joy dance on the breeze.
Squirrels prance in a playful race,
Chasing shadows, a merry embrace.

Branches sway with a soft delight,
As the day turns from dull to bright.
Laughter echoes, a light-hearted song,
Nature's symphony, where we all belong.

Beneath the ferns, delightful charades,
Unseen creatures in playful cascades.
Each rustle hints at a giggling sprite,
In this kingdom, everything feels right.

Sunset arrives, painting the sky,
The whispers fade, but spirits fly.
Evening wraps with a twinkling grin,
In this laughter, the heart doth win.

Glee in the Woodland Shadows

Under the canopy, shadows play,
Mischief found in the light of day.
Bouncing branches, the wind's delight,
Every step feels like taking flight.

A chorus of chirps and rustling leaves,
The secret tales that nature weaves.
Witty foxes in a midnight caper,
Chasing stars with a daring paper.

As dusk falls, the giggles expand,
Filling the air like grains of sand.
Moonlight tickles the forest ground,
In every corner, smiles resound.

Jokes of owls in their nightly prime,
Echo through the trees, a joyous rhyme.
With laughter woven through each branch,
In the woods, we all take a chance.

Fancies in the Ferns

Tiny critters in a tangled dance,
Every flutter gives hope a chance.
Bright-eyed bunnies with a cheeky hop,
From the high grass, they never stop.

Ferns sway, as if sharing jest,
In their midst is where hearts rest.
Crickets sing their nightly song,
While the stars wink and hum along.

A gust blows the petals in a spin,
Creating laughter within their grin.
The forest floor, a canvas of cheer,
With whispers of wonder that all can hear.

Fancies sprout from the ground below,
In every inch, good vibes will grow.
Embrace the fun where shadows gleam,
In nature's arms, we're all part of the dream.

Chuckles in the Hushed Hollow

In the hollow where secrets seem,
A playful brook flows like a dream.
Bubbles giggle as they race and twirl,
Casting ripples in a merry whirl.

The old trees bend, as if to laugh,
Sketching smiles on the wooden path.
Toads croak jokes from their mossy seat,
Each croak a word, each word a treat.

Breezes breeze through the quiet grove,
Encouraging tales of mischief and love.
Beneath the moon, friendships ignite,
In this hollow, everything feels right.

Rustling leaves tell stories grand,
Of joy and wonder in this land.
As the night wraps us in its keeps,
The chuckles linger in our dreams.

Revelry Rooted in Nature's Embrace

In the shade, where shadows dance,
The squirrels prance, they take a chance.
With acorns tossed, a merry spree,
Their giggles echo, wild and free.

The breeze brings whispers, soft and light,
As blossoms sway, what a funny sight!
The rabbits hop with joyful might,
In nature's joy, they find delight.

A sneaky fox plays peek-a-boo,
With twitching tails, he joins the crew.
The grasshoppers leap, a comic show,
In every corner, laughter flows.

Beneath the trees, the shadows stretch,
As nature's jesters find their sketch.
Their antics spark a lively cheer,
In forest realms, fun is always near.

Chortles Among the Canopies

The branches sway, a ticklish breeze,
With playful nudges, all at ease.
A parrot's squawk, a joyful sound,
As jesters in feathers spin around.

Chipmunks chatter, planning schemes,
Their little plots burst at the seams.
The owls wink with wise surprise,
In the dim light, fun never dies.

A raccoon grins as he stumbles,
While sleepy bees forget their fumbles.
The sun paints gold on foolish games,
With giggly echoes, nature claims.

The canopy sings, a chorus bright,
Tales of joy blend day with night.
Each leaf a stage for playful quests,
Where laughter shines, and spirit rests.

Mirthful Murmurs of the Meadow

In fields so wide where daisies gleam,
The breezes float like laughter's dream.
The butterflies twirl, a dance they share,
With nature's giggles filling the air.

The kittens chase their shadows round,
While bumblebees buzz, joy unbound.
A meadowlark sings a playful tune,
Inviting all 'neath the smiling moon.

The flowers sway, they sway so bold,
With stories of fun, forever told.
As laughter bursts from every hue,
Mirth's soft whispers ring so true.

The rabbits hop, the grass will bend,
With silly games that never end.
Together they weave a tapestry bright,
In the meadow's heart, pure delight.

Whimsy Wind-Tales in the Wildwoods

Within the woods where shadows twine,
The trees are storytellers, divine.
With whispers soft and breezy fun,
Each tale is spun beneath the sun.

An otter slides with joyful grace,
While turtles join, a sluggish race.
The spiders weave their silken art,
Crafting laughter that won't depart.

The rustling leaves are giggling too,
As frolicking squirrels perform their coup.
The gnomes dance 'round the toadstool ring,
In nature's ball, they always sing.

The wind hums tunes of quirky fate,
In every nook, fun congregates.
As twilight falls, the forest glows,
With whimsy tales that life bestows.

Playful Echoes Through the Thicket

In the woods, a giggle plays,
Frolicking whispers in sun's warm rays.
Branches sway in a gleeful dance,
Beneath the canopy, a merry prance.

Squirrels chime in, with cheeky flair,
Chasing shadows without a care.
Their antics spark chuckles all around,
In every nook, a joy is found.

Hiccups of laughter in soft rustling air,
Nature's jests, beyond compare.
Each rustle a smile, a playful tease,
Mirthful echoes among the trees.

The brook joins in with a bubbly tone,
Sharing secrets, not meant to be shown.
Together they weave a whimsical tale,
In thickets of joy, where spirits sail.

Smirks Under the Leafy Dome

A leaf flutters down with a cheeky grin,
It knows the fun that lies within.
Caterpillars chuckle, emerald on green,
In a world where the silly is often seen.

Under the canopy, shadows play,
Whispers of mischief fill the day.
Bumblebees buzz with a playful tune,
While butterflies dance, a colorful swoon.

A spider weaves jokes in its silky thread,
Spinning stories that lighten the dread.
The wind giggles through branches so high,
Carrying jests that float through the sky.

With every rustle, a punchline revealed,
In this leafy realm, no heart remains sealed.
Smirks abound in this vibrant muse,
Under a dome where laughter ensues.

Joyful Riffs of the Breezy Canopy

Up above, the leaves sway in cheer,
Whispers of fun dance in your ear.
Light-hearted melodies flutter and play,
In a symphony of joy that brightens the day.

The sun peeks through with a wink so bright,
Casting shadows that leap in delight.
Every rustle seems keen to confide,
Jokes of nature are caught in the tide.

Frogs croak out their own brand of fun,
While chattering mice enjoy the run.
With every flutter, a giggle is tossed,
In this playful grand, no moment is lost.

A breeze brings tales from the heights above,
Of creatures who share a pure kind of love.
In this canopy's heart, laughter takes flight,
Joyful riffs echo into the night.

Banter Among the Dancing Leaves

Amid the foliage, chortles arise,
As branches engage, beneath sunny skies.
Casting jests as the breezes sway,
Joy erupts in the liveliest way.

A raccoon flashes a comedic smirk,
While chipmunks chirp, in mischief they lurk.
Here, each glance ignites a smile,
Banter flows through woods, mile after mile.

Pinecones tumble like playful blights,
Causing sunsets to crumble in light.
Every shadow holds a chuckling friend,
In this merry old wood where giggles transcend.

Swaying branches sing along the line,
Offering jests as the stars align.
In this leafy refuge, all worries flee,
Together they thrive, in pure harmony.

Nature's Laughter Echoes Far and Wide

In the meadow, frogs wear hats,
As butterflies dance with little chats.
Squirrels drop acorns, making a mess,
While the wind giggles, feeling no stress.

Sunbeams tickle the flowers' toes,
As daisies whisper all that they know.
Crickets chirp with a silly tone,
And the world feels like a comedy zone.

Trees sway gently, swaying in glee,
While bees buzz jokes, oh so carefree.
Every rustle is a call to play,
In nature's theater, come what may.

With each giggle, the sky turns bright,
As shadows dance in sheer delight.
The earth, a stage for merry sound,
Where joy and whimsy can be found.

Celestial Chuckles from the Canopies

Up above, a crow wears a crown,
While pine trees sway, never feeling down.
Raccoons play dress-up, what a sight,
Their little antics fill the night.

The moon winks down with a silvery grin,
As stars burst forth in a gleeful spin.
Clouds share secrets, giggling so loud,
In this lofty world, no room for proud.

Fireflies sparkle like tiny lights,
Playing tag on warm summer nights.
The rustling leaves join in the fun,
With each chuckle, the day is done.

A twilight serenade, so divine,
As all the critters begin to rhyme.
From the branches high, joy does soar,
In nature's laughter, who could want more?

Folly and Frolic in the Fronds

In ferns, there's mischief, what a tease,
As lizards race, aiming to please.
A butterfly slips, landing in mud,
The giggles echo, the laughter's a flood.

Pigeons strut like they own the park,
While grasshoppers jump, creating a spark.
Cracked walnuts roll, a playful show,
As each critter takes a bow, nice and slow.

Sunflowers giggle, heads all a-turn,
In their bright laughter, the world can learn.
The babbling brook joins in their cheer,
Singing sweet music for all to hear.

The air is filled with whimsy and glee,
As magic swirls from tree to tree.
Every day a fest of pure delight,
In this lively realm, everything's bright.

Happy Heartbeats in the Leafy Labyrinth

In the garden maze, a rabbit hops,
Chasing his shadow, he never stops.
Bouncing on petals, soft and sweet,
With twinkling eyes and happy feet.

The hedgehog rolls, a spiny ball,
As daisies chuckle, answering the call.
Ladybugs boast with a gentle laugh,
Guiding the way, a silly path.

Under the canopy, giggles pop,
As butterflies twirl, they can't be stopped.
Each rustling leaf holds a secret gesture,
Of nature's humor, a wondrous treasure.

With each heartbeat, the joy expands,
As critters frolic in sun-kissed lands.
In the labyrinth green, smiles abide,
Where fun is the journey, joy is the ride.

Revelry Among the Roots

In the shade where shadows play,
Squirrels dance in bright array.
A rabbit prances by with flair,
Who knew woodland critters care?

Whispers tickle through the air,
Laughter echoes everywhere.
The brook giggles, splashing light,
Nature's jesters, pure delight.

Beneath the ferns, a fox does grin,
His antics make the birds all spin.
Clumsy beetles trip in line,
Nature's jesters feel divine.

The roots draped low, a festooned seat,
Where all the forest friends do meet.
With winks and nods, they share a tale,
In this laughter-filled woodland trail.

Joyful Secrets of the Glade

Mushrooms giggle in the shade,
Telling tales of mischief made.
A hedgehog rolls, a hapless sight,
While fireflies twinkle, laughter bright.

The breezy whispers weave a song,
In this glade where all belong.
Dancing leaves in jolly cheer,
Unmasking secrets, drawing near.

Frogs in chorus croak and clap,
Finding rhythms in the sap.
The owls hoot from their high throne,
As friendship blooms, never alone.

With every rustle, a fragrant joke,
As vine and flower tease and poke.
In the heart of green delight,
A world revels, pure and bright.

The Amusement of Rustling Petals

Petals flutter, pinks and golds,
Whispers soft, their tale unfolds.
The breeze joins in with ticklish glee,
Tickling blooms like a jolly spree.

Bumblebees buzz with a crooked grin,
Spinning tales of pollen in.
Caterpillars wiggle, tease and bend,
In this mirthful garden, laughter blends.

Butterflies wear their finest dust,
Flitting about, they laugh and trust.
The daisies giggle, twirl and sway,
In the sunlight, brightening the day.

From the petals, a symphony rings,
A chorus of nature, joy it brings.
With each rustle, each dance, each sigh,
The garden's alive, beneath the sky.

Delight in the Dappled Sunlight

Sunbeams sneak through leafy streams,
Playing tricks and weaving dreams.
Dancing shadows, a playful crew,
Tickling the ground anew, anew.

The chatter of crickets fills the space,
Matching the sun's warm embrace.
Chasing tails of lizards fast,
In this joy, we're tightly cast.

The playful winds call out with zest,
As little creatures join the fest.
Pinecone hats on squirrels' heads,
As laughter echoes 'round their beds.

Dappled sunlight finds its way,
To sprinkle mirth where youngsters play.
In every nook and every glen,
Nature's giggle, time and again.

Joyful Rustle in the Understory

In shadows dance the whispers bright,
A squirrel steals a snack in flight.
Worms wiggle with a giggly tease,
As breezes play and tickle trees.

A toad sings loud with pride and flair,
While bugs parade without a care.
The laughter of the brook nearby,
Bouncing jokes from soft blue sky.

Each rustle holds a silly phrase,
From leafy friends in sunny haze.
The ground is ripe with playful cheer,
Where all the plants are grinning here.

So join the fun, don't be aloof,
In nature's merry, jesting roof.
With every turn, a jest unfolds,
In whispers bright and stories told.

Serenades of Laughter through Branches

The branches hum a jolly tune,
As chipmunks bop beneath the moon.
Acorns drop with miniature thuds,
Creating giggles from the buds.

A parrot squawks with comic flair,
While dancing leaves swirl in the air.
The barky dogs bark soft and sweet,
Their grassy humor can't be beat.

A rabbit hops on sticky ground,
With every bounce, more chuckles found.
The world around is full of glee,
Where harmony meets jubilee.

So raise a cheer, let spirits soar,
In leafy laughter evermore.
For nature's stage is set tonight,
With joyous notes that feel so right.

Grins and Giggles in the Glade

The glade erupts with sprightly cheer,
Where whispers swap from ear to ear.
A fox jests with a flash of tail,
While fireflies blink a glow-y trail.

Mushrooms caper in a row,
With silly hats to top the show.
Clouds above giggle as they drift,
Creating joy, a charming gift.

Under the arch of emerald boughs,
Laughter bubbles from the cows.
Each rustle sings a merry jest,
In nature's lull, we find our rest.

So prance about, let fables grow,
In whimsical winds that twist and blow.
For here in shade, the mood's just right,
To share more jokes and feel the light.

Playful Spirits in the Leafy Realm

In tangled greens where fun prevails,
A caper sounds through leafy trails.
The wind whispers secret larks,
While tree trunks giggle at the barks.

Frolicsome ferns wiggle and sway,
With every nudge, they steal the day.
The berries blush in shy delight,
As shadows play with purest light.

A dancing leaf, a twirling breeze,
Inviting all to join with ease.
The playful twigs snap jokes around,
As laughter rises from the ground.

So leap and twirl in leafy glee,
For every twist brings joy, you see.
Embrace the fun with open hearts,
In nature's realm, where laughter starts.

www.ingramcontent.com/pod-product-compliance
Lightning Source LLC
Chambersburg PA
CBHW051630160426
43209CB00004B/585